The Orangery

The University of Texas Press Poetry Series, No. 3

The Orangery
Gilbert Sorrentino

University of Texas Press
Austin and London

Library of Congress Cataloging
in Publication Data
Sorrentino, Gilbert.
    The orangery.
    (The University of Texas Press
    poetry series; no. 3)
    1. Sonnets, American. I. Title.
PS3569.O707 811'.5'408 77-13099
ISBN 0-292-76008-6
ISBN 0-292-76009-4 pbk.

Grateful acknowledgment is made to
the following for permission to publish
these poems:

Black Sparrow Press: "Remember the story
of Columbus and the orange?"; "La Vie
d'Art"; "After Montale"; "King Cole";
"White Lemons"; "O Xmas tree"; "Silent
Knight"; "Arthur Rimbaud"; "Aesthe-
tics"; "Partial Graph"; "Everybody would
soon change"; "Zukofsky"; "She whom
no one ever found"; "She was all in
black. A statement"; "In Memoriam
P.B."; "1939 World's Fair"; "Seminar";
"Canta Naranja"; "Broadway! Broad-
way!"; "Now. Tell me how much I am to
respect"; "Across this water sits a shore";
"Chez Macadam"; copyright 1976 and
1977 by Gilbert Sorrentino, and pub-
lished in *A Dozen Oranges* and *White
Sail* by Black Sparrow Press.

Canto (Fall 1977): "Annie from Miami";
"Variations 3"; "Mr. America last seen
crossing the road"; "Je connais gens de
toutes sortes"; "At twenty love disinte-
grates."

Columbia (Fall 1977): "The white rockers
on the porch."

New Directions in Prose and Poetry 32:
(1976): "1939 World's Fair"; "Across this
water sits a shore"; "In Memoriam P.B.";
"Now. Tell me how much I am to re-
spect"; "Broadway! Broadway!"; "She
was all in black. A statement"; "She
whom no one ever found"; "Canta
Naranja."

New Directions in Prose and Poetry 35 (Fall
1977): "One Negative Vote"; "Footnote";
"Variations 1"; "The Mansion of the
Moon"; "Variations 2"; "White moons are
blank, blank moons"; "That the mouth
speak not daggers"; "To Sulpicia"; "Lone
Star"; "The Oranges Returned."

Sun & Moon 1 (1976): "Seminar" (called
"Orange Sonnet").

Text (1977): "Saying the Beads"; "Hom-
age to Arnaut"; "Nadie come naranjas";
reprinted from *Text*, issue no. 1, edited
by Mark Karlins.

To Vicki and Chris
"the Orange bright"

Contents

The Orangery

I still hear those azure carillons
floating from the Belgium building
caroming off the Trylon

and the Perisphere. Magic land.
Herr Dreyer grumbled because there was no
swastika. In "Florida" fake orange trees.

    My mother was beautiful
    in the blue gloom.
    How she loved me.

    Sore feet and headaches
    Depression and loneliness
    dulled her soft bloom.

She died ice-grey in Jersey City
with no solitary word.

Everybody would soon change
or die. Sudden burst
of my mother's youth revealed
when I was ten.

Thin dreams of my "new life"—
gone, gone. Thank God
all dreams are rubbish.
If they were not? A smell of rose oil.

I see her clear in a white dress
dear woman. The mist on Jersey fields.

Potato chips and orange drink
in the cool taproom
of the Warren House
thrilling summer afternoons.

The young man in khakis
sits on the quay hot
in the odd silence
of the Christmas Day.

    A certain light.
    Yellow saturated evaporating
    into whiteness far over
    the blue glint of the Gulf.

Mobile. The very name
a sunny orange sound.

    That there were roses
    in the garden. A rose of a house.
    That there were lime trees.

Smiles, scattered amid green. Rhodōnia.

Wham! Bam! Alla Kazam!
Nonsense words in a foolish song.
Its title all that has
value.
And that value is but a message
carried over time.
And also foolish.

It denotes a sky colored orange.
Not the sky nor its color
holds the value. In a mysterious
way these words (this "image"
mean something else.
Wham! Bam! Alla Kazam!
Fruitless.

On the side of a road in Alabama
an old Ford parked
the passengers here and there
in a field of white—

    These people arrested
    have only their surfaces
    to present yet they are clear
    as characters in—

Here and there in the field
in the pale moonlight a man
a woman two children
stilled in a drama that—

    They are eating something.
    Oranges. In a kind of beaten glamour.

Simplicity

Once when we were younger
fifteen years ago I in tie
and jacket you in a black dress
we took the wrong train

and had to run in a cruel
sun flaming reddish orange
for the right train on
another platform sweating

with luggage and I had
a bag of pots and pans. You
seemed miles in front of me
and I ran clanging. Wait!

Now we know this
and no one else knows anything.

A wanting. A desire.
The current cant is "needs."
What does one need
to live?

Ah but what does one
desire? Submerge the ego
in the image of a knight.
Alone and noble in the cold.

That curious thing named love.
Allow the man to hang some fragment
of himself on it, a phony orange
on an aromatic Xmas tree.

My Xmas tree. My Xmas tree.

Accept this shoddy decoration.

. . . all right. Faint sounds
of a trumpet and bees
swarming in the oak trees.

The orange twilight
gleams on this shell on which
a volcano smokes serenely.

A coin embedded
in a chunk of lava
also gleams

Holding down a few
sheets of paper
on the desk.

Life that once seemed so immense
Is less than your handkerchief.

The building had better days.
Immured in a situation "symbolized"
by orange.
I mean, it saw better days.

God only knows
what the rest of us saw. I know
what I saw. There was
certainly a roadhouse or two.

Off the highway orange drink
and cool Maria Elena. Afternoon
stilled in a smile
and a current pop tune.

I have decided this in the last minute.
It is as true as true.

Black streets a black
slick a black sheen and in
his heart.

That famous state
with its single star
as emblem.

It has an odd and silent
coast thick with limes
and roses.

Women in black muttering
their beads and Jesus
angles of pain.

There the sky clicks blue to black
here icy peach and orange almost blend.

Bluebonnets in Texas in a cold spring.
The sky over them as blue as blue.
In a small arroyo near San Antone
a Spaniard builds a limetree fire.
This man comes from Amarillo
which exists in pale orange light
luminous in the thin blue air.

He sings: I heard the blue bells
of Sevilla banging the yellow air
ay! ay! The air in Amarillo
is not yellow but is blue. The blaze
bursts high in a cracking orange flame.
A blue Buick passes by in dusty clouds
and a blonde therein laughs toward Laredo.

Straight down from Amarillo
rattled Betsy Pink and Mexicali Rose
in an (past mesquite and stunted willow)
 old black Ford
they stopped for icy orangeade
and sensuously dawdled in the shade
while sunlight shimmered on their sheerest hose.

Their summer frocks were palest lime and yellow
and bored Parisienne manquée their pose
as they clattered off in their mellow
 old black Ford
bleached Paint Rock was bitterly dismayed
as señoritas stopped but never stayed
the dust and grit but rose and rose and rose.

Nothing whatever to see
There. Where in memory I see sleet.

   Thus ending and the day turns

Brilliant February.

         Thus ending, her life ending.
         With no carillons
         Neither orange trees.

Light flashing brilliant on ice.
There must be
                  rose gardens somewhere in this town.

Nothing to see. In coma. Then gone.
As youth has also gone
         bells of high requiem.

Stupid play. That thinks things are all right.

The bente moone with hire hornes pale
is loose in heaven.

    With her face averted the woman
    tends her roses.
    Her pale hands.

We can almost see right through the moon
that perfect blue. Delicate coin
our only perfect silver.

This fresh white silver
with her pale horns, pale
and the woman stares now past
the lime trees past the orange glare.

    Her white features assert themselves
    —it is an icy composition.

Who
was that who
saw
his father
in
his shorts,
mother laughing?

Who
decided on
the
pattern?
Of
oranges?
On white.

Who was that?
Who
saw his father?
In his shorts!
Mother
laughing.
Who?

Who
decided?
On the
pattern of
oranges
on
white.

The sun has set and the sea
is calm now. I am with
my shadow on the beach
and the sea is barely murmuring.

    Faint orange wash still
    in the sky and soon Orion
    will stalk through the dark
    and I apace with him.

My heart in my dark breast
is murmuring songs from long ago
white words that stand clear
in the vague light. I can hear
the voices of the girls light
on the air. Completely alone.

She whom no one ever found
death found in Jersey City.

    Monsieur Mort, in a stupid play
is a Frenchman of perfect grace.
Politely he refuses orange ice
with vanilla ice cream crowning it.

    He prefers crème glacée, eh? He
smoketh Gauloises and Gitanes.

    In the "film" they make of it
the plot is slightly warped.
Still, the gent simpers on and on
about his business. You know.

    All in black with a French accent.
Plenty of crackling wit.

Did you ever hear mission bells
ringing? Pull down thy vanity!
Did you ever see brightness
fall from the air, Mexicali Rose?

Went down to the ships, mission
bells all brightness. Mexicali
Rose beneath the paper moon.
All in the air is vanity.

The moon growing dim the moon
a brightness in the air. The moon orange
in its flight its light upon
a field of white and snowy cotton.

Her heart beat bright hammer
O Rose! Your big brown eyes.

Halloween is black and orange.
A song, as in "le clarinet du marmalade."
Some are happiest drowned
in a saxophone solo.

"Le jazz hot" rhymes à la Mallarmé
with tabasco: *vide* Bunk Johnson
astomp in New Iberia.

I saw Dexter Gordon play to six people
in a frayed suit. His golden horn had lost
its sheen. The notes gleamed.

Dexter in his brilliance.
Exquisite phrasing and perfect comedy.
A black velvet an
orange corona corona.

Remember the story of Columbus and the orange?
He impressed Isabella with a demonstration.
King Ferdinand thought it a sensation.
But nothing rhymes with orange.

I see him turning that fruit in his hand
So that the whole globe, seas and all, was orange.
Now the only thing that's orange
Seems the bloody North of Ireland.

With nothing up my sleeve I rhyme with orange.
Note well the swift flutter of the letters.
As in: "There once lay a lady of letters."
With nothing in my head I rhyme with orange.

The image "clarinet marmalade" is black and orange.
Auditor dixit: "A poem! Not this boring orange!"

How odd that they have this orange hair
to go with their cruel northern faces
set in a kind of fixed intelligence
that writes no poems God help us.

They go down to the sea with those faces
that orange hair calling to us to come come
all bag and baggage and with sighs of thanks
to their dead northern places.

Northern races are intelligent and know
of space they say their orange hair
shocks us gleaming in the frigid light
that skates upon a white and frozen sea.

Going down going down going down
to the sea. Welcome! Cruel water.

Across this water sits a shore
patched together out of dim and smudgy colors.
It brings to mind a cartoon oddly porous.
Static on a worn-out sponge. Yet a core
of translucent light seems to spring
from the center of what looks a town or market
and drenches the lime-green haze of the park
I put there. One seesaw, one fountain, and one swing.

Mothers and children in blue
filled with good humor, china blue
eyes and the rest, plus the sky is blue.

You can see I'm trying to get there
seriously. When I get there
I'll be young again. I forgot orange. There.

Lavender, vanilla, anything.
The belt worn with such elegance
by the Mydas fly.

How still. How still.
Dusk ever. The rosy bridge.
Everything is almost perfect
In its name.

I give you the coronet, dead man.
Wear it in health. I never dream of you.
Vanilla. Orange ice. Un sombrero.
A lavish sunset soaks Brooklyn
With excruciating love.

Kings. Kings. Kings. Kings.

Ah! The streets of dream

The sweet of dreams
is a Mexican Hat.
The sweet of dreams
a sombrero.
A sweet of dreams
on the street of dreams.
Canta no lloro.

The sweet of dreams
is an orange hat.
The sweet of dreams
has vanillo.
One dreams of the sweet
on the street of dreams.
Ay! Ay! Perdido.

Mr. America last seen crossing the road
in a cloud of Rum and Maple smoke.

His hair gives off the scent of eau de Rose
and the late sun finds out his white shoes.

His burnt-orange slack suit glows
with an elegance precisely mellow.

A woman in a dress a spanking white
releases an enamel smile.

She has a white rose in her teeth no guile
flickers in her wide azure eyes.

Her hair is blond she dies she dies
inside for love for love has died.

He boards the train in cindery smoke.
The sun the color of her dress now. White.

No one could enter those vast fields
of snowy cotton but the elect.

In the cascades of moonlight
they performed their rites.

There were kisses and whispered words
on the Alabama breeze.
In this candor another candor
of private mysteries.

The subtleties of magnolia
and honeysuckle of orange blossoms
borne on the air from
the south. Hammered by the light.

Their hearts careened with the falling
stars falling in glamorous silence.

Black, ice-grey, white, azure, orange,
cities, clinics, snows, and saxophones.

There are certain birds in backyards
whose chirps and cries I never liked.

Poor dandelions too and daisies,
black-eyed Susans, Queen Anne's lace.

The clarinet soft from out the roses
pitched clear nodes, rhodōnia.

Clutter of flowers I proffer to
clutter of colors, yet save one.

The magic flower whose fruit is love
l'absente de tous bouquets

And whose seed is joy whose scent
destroys ennui.

White moons are blank. Blank moons
over Córdoba are blanco. Yet
when Flaubert looked up he saw the
same moon blanc. These things prove
that rhyme is necessary.

For instance a dance
is a stance
in movement. It changes.
Take the movies. Oranges.
The girl's a pearl.

> Spanking white paint
> albus ain't.
> Dark gold of an orange
> held by Candida.

She was all in black. A statement
to take its place in "The History of Ideas."

We know black here in America.
Why, it's a scream.

Stick a point of orange in it
just for fun. Just to see what comes of it.

    After which: Prove that the light
    of bowling alleys is romantic.
    Is the very gravy of romance.
    "The crème!" yells a voice.

    Then, years later, drones the comic,
    I recall standing on a corner
    in the Bronx waiting for a bus.
    Yes, yes. Waiting for a bus.

Black, blank, vermillion, green and cobalt—
Where do you come from?
Do the birds invent you in their notes
morning and evening?

Orchards grey in morning mist—
Glitter and buzz of flies in sunlight—
I color my song, I color
my song—

The sunlight drenching the earth
sunlight compact in an orange ball
at evening. The flowers etched clear
in transparent light.

Do I find my heart in all of this?
(What is the question?) My red heart?

On the street that stands
in its single syllable right there
a subway kiosk. "Picture of the City."

A lamppost atop which a lighted
orange globe that shows the location
of a fire alarm box.

"Lamppost" could end a distich
of Catullus. Orange could end
up anywhere and does.

Poetry must not be poured into molds
the man said, fighting an old battle
filled with wild alarums.

No one eats oranges
in anybody's poems.

When the moon sails out
the bells are lost
the paths appear,
mysterious.

When the moon sails out
the sea includes the land
the heart becomes
an island in the infinite.

> No one eats oranges
> under the full moon.
> One eats of needs
> the green and icy fruit.

When the moon sails out with a hundred perfect faces
Dimes and nickels sob in your pocket.

Her pale horns immaculate
over Kings.

    High and vague
    in the washed-out blue

almost invisible.

Purity of water despite this filth.
Profligate scatter of sunshine yellow
and white and orange.

    Is it the moon? Is it
    the moon? Is that
    the moon? Is it the
    moon? The moon? The moon?
    Up there is that the moon?
    The moon? The moon? The moon.

Locked away by choice this billionaire
who is no eccentric but has made his own
time. He supposes.

This curious regimen may be considered
weird, an odd artistic devotion that makes
nothing. Rises in black night.

A movie. Television. A quart of orange
juice. Three chocolate puddings. Another
movie. Phone calls.

Sleeps in the fierce daylight in dreams
of Dustin Hoffman and Faye Dunaway. A thin
slice of the moon shows. He rises.

Poached eggs on white toast. Reads of
the contest winner who dreams of Kansas.

Dreams of Kansas.
City steaks.
Dead steers and flies.

Flies to Kansas City.
Dreams of steak.
The pilot steers down.

Who? The Kansas City
Kid. The steak city
scorches in the sun.

"Steers Dead in Sun":
Kansas City Messenger.
He disembarks to flies.

In the luncheonette a dead fly
in his orangeade.

That the mouth speak not daggers
but speak fire of which light
is its property. That the past
be not illumined but allowed

to blaze forth the brilliance
proper to it.

What is the past of orange?

    Oranged.

The orange's past is green
hard and sour, a plain fruit
splendid in its ripeness
as splendid in its salad days

      light amid the green daze
      of the groves

The pale moon sails out blank.
Green fruit in the trees and
in the green trees oranges.
They are limes they

are oranges. The n is a kind
of fly that lands on
nothing. The birds flash
in morning silver light.

    Glitter and buzz of.
    the transparent.
    flash of green.

    handful of silver coins
    caught by the girl the
    comedienne, Madame Mystère.

Certain odd emblems are needed
to freshen the spirits. This
was delivered with no tone

one grey afternoon by a man
on a corner in the Bronx.
He had a wax nose, baggy

pants. Je dis: une fleur!
a man said, the words thin
in cold vapor. Flowers

remind me of funeral homes
Raymond Banal off from work
moonlighted. Then, the comic

said, What about some Oranges?
Golden Lamps in a green Night?

She had on a sweet vermillion gown,
Sue, the strange comedienne.
Everyone loved her, why,
even the birds sang for joy
when she swallowed the orange.

Her routine with the wax orange
was a spectacle of utter joy.
How she did it and why,
well, the queen comedienne
just smiled and smoothed her gown.

Sue, sweet Sue, a gracious interview
given to loving cameras. She was swank
and svelte and answered the questions
thus: blankety blank blank blank.

On the tropical coast of Java
Arthur Rimbaud watched movies
an odd sight in his bluchers
and his orange sombrero.

He said: An excellent jelly: guava?
to an audience of weary floozies
con men thieves and moochers.
He snapped the brim of his sombrero.

He wrote: This island once was lava
to Jeans Pierres and Suzies.
Four were drunks, two butchers.
Sun glanced off his sombrero.

He returned sans medals lucre
or poetry. Lost his sombrero.

In love with grand designs
some say
Rimbaud was a blue-eyed devil.
Across the wide Missouri

Others say that
oranges are good for you
See: "Italy"
Roll Missouri roll

From the gallery (what gallery?)
we hear
Arthur was a sweet and holy child
O Shenandoah

O roll across the wide Missouri
Sweet Shenandoah roll

Is the eye interested in
color or the lack of it?
Is black a color or how about white?
Who remembers Art Appreciation?

"The Blue Boy" is Freddie Bartholomew.
(Can the eye be said to be "interested"?
Black and white whatever they say
is always chic.

But "chic" says Baudelaire is
a memory of the hand and not the mind.
(Can the hand be said to have a memory?
Who really knew Charles Baudelaire?

Rimbaud sailed away on the Prince of Orange.
Did he know Baudelaire? (His blue-white eye

In Paris where the rue de la Nuit
meets the gold of the day
there is a small café La Vie en Rose
all of whose red-and-white tablecloths
have vases holding tiny roses

A woman with green eyes
in a black silk dress
often sips a bock there
and when I pass beneath the chestnuts
our eyes embrace in French

As this woman is Floridian
her hair is a glowing orange
I take an orange from my jacket pocket
the lady and I trade white smiles

When in Paris do as the Parisians do
it will get you nowhere.

They do not seem to care
about the purity of your intent.

On the other hand they are content
anent their ignorance of Florida.

They think it is a humid bog
where gators feed on oranges.

This idée fixe of Florida is bent
as to both form and content.

You say "Its purity! Its swell intent!"
It is their vin for which they care.

Yet if you do as the Parisians do
in Paris it will get you nowhere.

Paris moon-drowned streets and the chestnuts blooming
silver thighs aglow and black eyes are drunken
limes and roses flash they are blue and mauve here
    oranges glowing.

Alabama Nights the café with green wine
welcomes foreign flesh "la chanteuse Lingerie"
croons "bip boom boom boom" in her silks and laces
    orchestra blowing.

Now the yellow gloom of the cave gets brighter
tables groan the tone of a sigh is lucent
golden gin with mint is the drink preferred by
    Madame Mystèro.

Soon that tropical lady tells of doomed love
    platinum starlight.

Now. Tell me how much I am to respect
the Prince of Orange. In that fine-spun prose
that fine-spun rosy prose.

How sheen it is! (Talk of dopey Raggedy Ann
hanging from a peg is talk
stained purple from sour grapes.

So they say. What a fine ring
(or is it twang?) the word "frivolous"
possesseth. Yea.

About dead Arthur. Who knows but I
that he loved licorice and
marshmallows?

Not you swell fellows and girls no no
Nor you swell girls and fellows

The King of the dark tower is a lug.
Although we like your book we have
no money. Have a drink? Dinner?

Dinner is duelos y quebrantos.
Although I grow more remote I stay
out of the ivory tower.

The angels in the sky the angels
hover just outside my tower hover
in placid gusts from Miami Beach.

They know where their bread is buttered
and why not? Are they not for the most
part manes? Sweet faces and milk songs.

Duelos y quebrantos? Is this the same city
Diamond Jim's apéritif was a gallon of o.j.?

Gold and oranges
golden oranges, out of Persia
bouquets of orange blossoms.

Who are these exotics
dazed and narcotized
by Orange Blossoms?

There is no Persia.
Those ghosts . . .
Varied comedians
claim the Bronx as home.

Though there is nothing sad
about those millions dead
there they are. Corpse upon corpse
breathing history to ghosts.

What is "the history of ideas"?
One orange.

And it deals with it how?
Six orange.

What of its silent "peripheries"?
Have a orange.

But do the intellectual?
Icy orangeades.

But can an idea actually live?
An orange dress.

Certainly, civilization can't.
Angelo's orange.
History! Forever fresh!
A tangelo's orange.

Those who like oranges are nice people.
These terrible people like oranges
And are terrible people.

Oranges can help nobody.
A man with a cold eats oranges.
He is suddenly cured.

Nice people secretly hate oranges.
The President loves them.
The President's wife says he's nice.

Terrible people hate the President.
They go mad for oranges.
Some think them garbage.

All Protestants are afraid of oranges.
Joe is a Protestant President.

(Joe is a Protestant President.)

Protestants often live beneath
the ginkgo tree says Mexicali Rose
with her absolute logic.

Mexicali Rose lives in Texas
where there are no ginkgos
where there are palms and limes.

Rose has some smile! And when
she cries it stays right there.
The President wrote her once.

The note went Rose O Rose
you are sweet you are fair
send me a carton of limes

send me an orange star send me
a lock of your ebony hair.

On the coast of Brooklyn
there were small ferries
in the shape of limes
their color too was green
they strolled through white down
and gun-grey waters carrying
no movie stars or Presidents
to Staten Island and then back
for there was nothing to be had
in those obscure boroughs
no orange groves or kliegs
to enunciate the famous smiles
practicing to sell us cars
and aspirin and wars and pekoe.

In a disingenuous letter
sent from a quiet snowy place
an old friend asks why I returned
    a gift of oranges.

I am too old to answer such questions.
Even the words sat numb. His was always
a brilliant mind yet he asks about
    his gift of oranges.

I put him in a poem once. God knows
he's had his slow shock in the mirror.
Perhaps it was that grey head sent
    the gift of oranges.

It is a maniac time, friends cast about
to touch. To reawaken. Meaningless gifts.

I know a lot of people who once seemed
fluid, one looked and saw them trying
to find a face and pose and freeze it.
Accessories to each other's surrender.

They had tics they had habits they knew
odd things about odd things, how they
misunderstood each other. They thought
the world a place to dance in.

When I see them as seldom as I can
they speak a perfect English that is
perfectly opaque: orange sled, Swiss
chard, gin in a jar, peachblow.

They are alive with old wives or new
pieces of them strewn across the city.

The white rockers on the porch
were drowned in the white light
their definition lost.

Old elms silent in the calm
and the birds too, silent. A woman
in orange slacks.

Ripped seats of the old Ford.
Cold water of the locks
of the old canal.

>Click of years. White smoke
>of a cigarette. New waters.
>The sun drenches everything.

>Click. High blue sky. All
>one chain of brilliant links.

1. Slid down the zeppelin and cut his rump
2. The back door opens   cold air   bottle of Worcestershire
3. Snow halfway up the door   the unpaved street
4. Dead in Jersey City   ruptured aneurism
5. Independence Day he "smokes" his grampa's pipe
6. Packards and broken hearts
7. Who   the toothy child in glasses   with an orange cat
8. Dead in Jersey City   freezing
9. Empty house he does not understand
10. The girl   the lake   the canoe
11. Girl   the lake   the cigarette   white smoke imagined
12. Dead in Jersey City   priest to whom he's civil
13. Do clinics build character   pimps of success say so
14. Dead in Jersey City   not one remark   speak   speak

Rosy. Azure.
There are no carillons
in Jersey City.
There are no carillons.
Who the subtle man
in the coronet?
The color of its gold
is almost orange.
Sparkle out in Queens!
That's the ticket.
Lavish against black.
Now the rose and azure black.
It seems a little late in the season
to have snow.

Frigid air
hauls sleet and freezing rain
from Canada the planes
and locusts of the neighborhood
are sticks of grey

The planes and locusts of
the neighborhood are
sticks of grey. Sleet from
Canada and rain. Freezing
rain

    orange love seems what it always was,
    impossible

    and orange, love, seems
    what it always was.

Are there new beginnings?

Outside that is of lying texts.

Old men die in bed alone wishing
for a drink in their dreams
leaving behind Christ knows what.
They are the ones who can hardly cross
the street their pants all baggy filth.

They cry with shame and delight
for a miserable dime they get that
putrid muscatel they fill their heads
with buzzing and crippled memory all
orange orange orange orange.

Christ knows what they leave behind.

See: "New Beginnings" in *A Lying Text*.

Ladies and gentlemen
a compact cat
and over here
an orange
and over here
some more
ladies and gentlemen

a perfect sphere
a kind of gold
direct from Persia
and over here
its missing n
batted by the cat
ladies and gentlemen

An orange some one
sat on one
end of a green orange.
Sat on this end of.

Perhaps it was a little
angel? It brought its
little jar of honey too.
Too honeyed words a little too
too melliflu

A rough sort of cone with
some bumps. Green with a
stem at the apex do you call it?
Call it any rough thing but don't
call it late for supper honey

O Xmas tree
still breathing in the bitter
grey December of 14th Street.

    It is but
    the living proof of love.

Perhaps he has not
tried his best. Tangle
of years.

    Will he now do
    that old soft shoe?

Soon it will burst out in spangles
of red blue green and orange light.

Against all reasonable thought
he wants. He prays it may blow green again.

To William Bronk

This cottony and juiceless orange is
this cottony and juiceless orange.
Of course.

What did one expect the world to be?
The world is eminently fair.
What a bitter taste that leaves.
If one could only rail against it.

If one could consider everything
as part of a scenario, some plan,
some convoluted narrative in which
all disasters have a perfect place.

But cruel idiots are rich. Mozart
is shoveled into the mud. Evil, with
its boring grin. All's fair. All's fair.

The rich man wanted breakfast.
He wanted coffee eggs bacon kippers
orange juice.

People in such situations are
not pitiable no matter how they
shout and bang the silver servers.

Big-breasted dowagers in comic strips
say in the face of this "My dear." That's
what they say: "My dear."

We all want that breakfast some time.
Even Lorca though he disguised his oranges
as lemons almost white.

Let him crash the silver for eternity.
Who? Him. Him? Who him? White lemons?

The finest gloom is always
edged with laughter. The finest
bloom. Every morning is
a brand-new day. Applause.
That's mah baby now.

    Yessir!
    That's mah baby.

If you don't like grapefruit
have some orange juice.
The sun is booming in the window.
Harumph! A brand-new day!
'Tis the blooming bloody berries.

    That is. You bet.
    Mah baby now.

Think they are old at 50
they all know each other.
Exquisite bunch of delegates
to the flower union.
See them among the posies.

Over here's a cabin where
the real people live. They look
at the real birds and the real pond
d-d-doin' that Walden Rag. Even the
orange juice comes out real by God.

How come they all know each other?
Hot dog! Those ham and eggs!

What you want's in a grain of sand.
Three times a day.

The fabled comedienne said
—she was not too fabled but she
looked swell in tights—what *did*
she say? Huh?

I know! She said that when you see
an orange sun sink slowly svelte slippery
behind those harsh ("harsh" is good) hills

. . . uh, uh, lost in the fog of time
what she said. But you can bet anyway
that given her supply of American trash
she knew that it was goddamned beautiful!

Yes suh! 'Twas also sunny and quiet
and in the shade of the old apple tree
everyplace is shit but here. Hut!

Over twenty centuries
her eyes find me
and I hear her voice.

    Lady, were you gratified?
    Soft mode of flutes
    woven with your singing.

I too am a poet
of the city.
Dulcius urbe quid est?

    That the Queen of Cythera
    keep her promise
    to you.

That the white wool of his toga
be bright as moonlit oranges.

Blue bells in the memory
a wash of blue lights a wash
over white artifacts

unlike the visage of Ozymandias
all are rubble. In America
the past lives in the mind.

It is not the beautiful
one wants to save but save it all.
Great grey glacier of my city.

Let all the nouns be testament.
Let them stand clear, reverberant.
This one and this one and this one.

These oranges hold it all. I love
my family my work. My captured city.

Dry crackle of leaves
blown erratically over the rusty grass.
Ice thin and fine a crystal
luminous in the bleached sunlight.
The birds are gone save for the blue dazzle
of the jays.

Thin smoke white against azure.
The roof tiles blue and ochre
across the lake. I stand alone
shivering in the wind
sweeping from the mountains.
Where is she?

> Where is she who gave me the orange
> from Persia in summer long ago?

Now here I proffer you, lecteur,
some good American, the harsh words
ice. And waste.

You can put them in your next
agreement, your next argument, you
can take them down to gaudy Florida.

Who remembers Florida? Ah.
The greeny groves, the sea, the lemons,
limes, the sun and grapefruit, oranges.
Platinum stars falling on its neighbor.

In some street in Miami Beach at night
set them down with care in moonlight.
The tropic air will set them free, take care
their gear includes ID and shoulder patch.

The harsh words ice and chaste
are good American, they sing
of death and winter, waste.

Frozen chics depart in haste
for Florida. (They don't bring
the harsh words, ice and chaste.)

Sun dumb, they smell and taste
fluffy orange frappes, here's nothing
of death and winter waste.

Cakes oozing with lime paste
yet in the news a chilling sting:
the harsh words Ice and Chaste.

Those harsh words: "ICE AND CHASTE."
"DEATH AND WINTER." "WASTE."

At twenty love disintegrates
with perfect ease. The phone
said no a letter no her knees
and mouth blurred.

When the rain lashed at the windows
all stupid songs seemed mysteries
and innocent items coats and rings
glowed with misery. In every city
the wind discovered me and in every wind
the burden of an idiot song.

I carried the pieces
I could find into many
an orange sunset even into
Baltimore and Waco.

They hauled him many times
from place to place
the black locomotives of the Erie

and the Delaware Lackawanna
and Western, the diesels
of the Penn and Santa Fe.

Why he went and where he got
bathed in a haze now.

Surely there was something
some duty or a bright smile?

Orange glare on the snow
outside Needles. Cinders
and mosquitoes in New Jersey.
Cold grey walls of Joliet.

A high blue sky clicks into place
soon after dawn. As usual millions
live and die beneath it.

Among them comics and comediennes
those who die for a laugh
but not for laughs. Enormous waste
seems to occur and reoccur.

As I grow older many of them persist
as ghosts encapsulate in persistent
scenes dreamy yet exact.

I see them all ugly smiles
or beloved smiles as they were
in snow in trolleys in new suits
as children eating orange ice.

This is a "brilliant" book!
This one not too "brilliant."
Note the bitterness and wanton
patterns of assault. Oh note.

This one used to be a poet.
You remember him?
Often he proves embarrassing however.
No matter what he does.

Something must have happened to him.
Perhaps his orgones ran away? Between
the lines the acute reader can read
there's love ripped with "something."

Anyhow. He's not open to life and
well, say Nature. He adds oranges and apples.

The rushing darkness of the summer evening.
Across the dirt road from the white farmhouse
a white wooden church its yard overgrown
with sweet grasses and in the dark blue air
the slow scribbling of the fireflies.
An old black Ford with stained grey seats
parked in the massing shadows the shadows
of two horses merge in a field of rye.
In an orange light in the dining room
a woman clears the supper dishes from the table.
Sweet voices of girls from the church steps
and muffled from inside the Ford thin
popular song resplendent with half-truths
and darkness, summer evening rushing.

1.

The smoke of an orange corona corona
releases the imagination so that
it lights upon that shady porch
on which white rockers gleam whiter
in the cool blue shadows and a woman
in orange slacks turns her head her face
composed but distant distant and you see
she doesn't know you her imagination dwells
on brown wavy hair and the scent of rose oil
departed.

Now the sunlight is compact in an orange ball
and she is alone there rocking rocking
O God! she murmurs to the emptiness.
Stares past lime trees past the orange glare.

2.

Stares past lime trees past the orange glare
into a garden. The comic sees a woman there
move amid spangles of red blue green
and orange light.

She tends her roses and her oranges
yet she is crying bitterly. He doffs
his orange hat and croons "Mexicali Rose"
yet she continues crying.

Do you remember, he says, our trip
to Florida? You were in a black dress
and we almost missed the train? I know.
I remember. No one else knows anything!

The lady feels a waft of that past glamour
the faint orange wash of thrilling voyages.

3.

The faint orange wash of thrilling voyages
had no possibility of existing
for my mother, striking in a white dress.

It was substituted for by azure carillons
chiming in the borough of Queens
of Depression and of coming war.

In her eyes the plea: Send me an orange star
went of course unheeded. This iron world
had forgotten all her photographs.

My concern was with vanilla and with orange ice
with the fake orange trees of "Florida."
With a Lincoln Zephyr the color of limeade.

She died ice-grey and silently in Jersey City
in February long before the orange twilight.

4.

In February long before the orange twilight
slathers an orange glare on the snow

dreams of Kansas possess him. He sees
in those dead white fields a woman

whose hair is a glowing orange
in a black silk dress impervious

to the bitter winds. She smiles
in French a white French smile

and unpacks a small embroidered bag
of tricks. She is the famed

Madame Mystère! late of Paris
by way of Emporia and points east.

He walks to her his brain an irregular verb.
La Mystère shakes up some Orange Blossoms.

5.

La Mystère shakes up some Orange Blossoms
places them on the table with a little jar
of honey and a bag of pots and pans.
Perhaps she does deserve the jeering.
Yet no one else certainly knows anything.
I mean: what do they know of magic
in Emporia or Amarillo?

Then Sue in her vermillion gown
comes on stage unwinding opaque jokes
and the room is stilled: some think of
orange sleds, some green nights, some marmalade.
A clarinet is playing and the past arrives
costumed as the spectre of a bum. Sue cracks:
"He is immured in a situation symbolized by orange."

6.

He is immured in a situation symbolized by orange.
No thrust will free him of it now, he knows.
He feels his heart to be the orange from Persia.
In summer, long ago, shooting stars
trailed platinum roaring toward Dixie.
    No one else knows anything, my love
    only we say "zeppelin."

Do you recall my clanging run
in the heat of July? my Wait?
the reddish orange of the cruel sun?
Where are my tie and jacket? your black dress?
My dear, no one else knows anything
    but we know this:
    Nothing is the thing that rhymes with orange.

7.

Nothing is the thing that rhymes with orange.
Who knows it knows it even in Laredo.
And in Laredo church bells chime and chime
until the brain surrenders.

 There the blonde in the Buick went
 to murmur of acceleration
 and orange twilight over Joliet.

How is it that I have come out here
where nothing rhymes with orange?
I have your photo in a black silk dress
wherein your face is mystery.

 These images persist snow crystals
 brilliant upon this iron world. Your face within
 the smoke of an orange corona. Corona.